nity

What Do
OFFICERS Do?

Nick Christopher

New York

Published in 2016 by The Rosen Publishing Group, Inc.
29 East 21st Street, New York, NY 10010

First Edition

Editor: Katie Kawa
Book Design: Katelyn Heinle

Photo Credits: Cover (police officer), p. 1 Blend Images - Hill Street Studios/Brand X Pictures/Getty Images; cover (hands) bymandesigns/Shutterstock.com; series back cover Zffoto/Shutterstock.com; pp. 5, 14 © iStockphoto.com/kali9; pp. 6, 21 John Roman Images/Shutterstock.com; p. 9 Peter Dazeley/Iconica/ Getty Images; pp. 10, 24 (uniform) pio3/Shutterstock.com; p. 13 © iStockphoto.com/shaunl; p. 17 Carolina K. Smith MD/Shutterstock.com; pp. 18, 24 (siren) Kant Komalasnangkoon/Shutterstock.com; p. 22 Karsten Bidstrup/Lonely Planet Images/Getty Images.

Library of Congress Cataloging-in-Publication Data

Christopher, Nick.
 What do police officers do? / Nick Christopher.
     pages cm. — (Helping the community)
 Includes bibliographical references and index.
 ISBN 978-1-4994-0656-6 (pbk.)
 ISBN 978-1-4994-0657-3 (6 pack)
 ISBN 978-1-4994-0658-0 (library binding)
 1. Police—Juvenile literature. I. Title.
 HV7922.C47 2016
 363.2—dc23
                                    2015000448

Manufactured in the United States of America

CPSIA Compliance Information: Batch #WS15PK: For Further Information contact Rosen Publishing, New York, New York at 1-800-237-9932

CONTENTS

Police officers help people
stay safe.

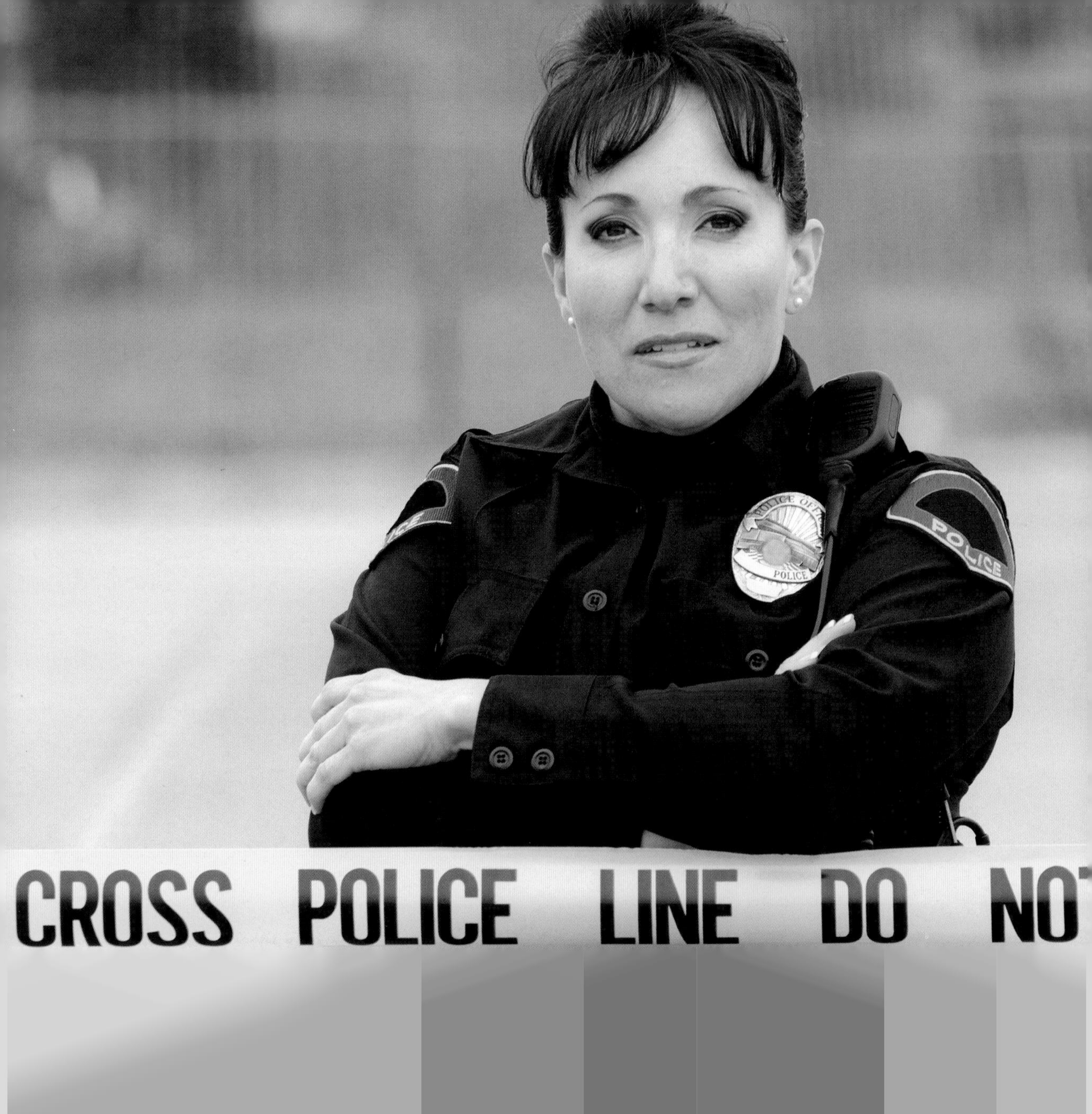
POLICE
POLICE
CROSS POLICE LINE DO NOT

Police officers make sure people follow laws. Laws are important rules.

Police officers also help kids who are lost.

Police officers wear clothes called a **uniform**.

Police officers drive cars
that can go fast!

Police officers stop people when they are driving too fast.

Police cars have lights on the top. The lights are red and blue.

SIREN

Police cars have a **siren**.
Sirens make loud noises.

Some police officers work with dogs.

Police officers are very helpful!

WORDS TO KNOW

siren

uniform

INDEX

WEBSITES

Due to the changing nature of Internet links, PowerKids Press has developed an online list of websites related to the subject of this book. This site is updated regularly. Please use this link to access the list: www.powerkidslinks.com/htc/pol